Wonky Fingers

Sarah Al-Hajj

BookLeaf Publishing

India | USA | UK

Presentation by *BookLeaf Publishing*

Web: www.bookleafpub.com

E-mail: info@bookleafpub.com

ISBN: 9789358315950

First edition 2023

DEDICATION

To the month of January.

PREFACE

On journeys, I often stare out the window, lost in the past and try to articulate what, at the time, felt unspeakable. This is a good time to mention I have no idea how to write a preface.
My main motivation for writing this collection was the desire to vocalise rushes of pure emotion and make them vivid. I adore the code-ridden language that is poetry and enjoyed writing with the purpose of encasing meaning within what was not said; every comma, space and line break was designed to satisfy all fellow poetry-nerds out there. Themes of love, loss, nature and healing are not at all new, but can now be experienced through one more writer, one more heart. There is some thematic continuity throughout the collection, and some poems do follow a 'natural progression' within a particular theme. That being said, many do not. The collection can be erratic, reflective of my impulsive fixations with the world's wonders. Rain, then bees, then bubbles, then the concept of impressions. The list goes on.
As with lots of contemporary poetry, this collection interacts with traditional forms, such as the sonnet, and reshapes it yet again. One

sonnet in the collection is about love, whereas the other is about drowning. The form is vulnerable to the stark contrasts of the selfless adoration of another being and the selfish desire to continue living for the sake of self-indulgence. 'How to press flowers (for poets) in less than eight steps' not only has numbered stanzas, and reads like instructions, but satirises the poetic medium itself, poking fun at academic attempts to find meaning in every letter. Similarly, 'sad girl poet' is horribly self-aware and mocks my tendency towards the love-sick. It is inserts like these which render a healthy balance between the grave and the unserious. Why should misery weigh down my love of sarcasm? Despite my self-ridicule, this was a genuine fear I had approaching publishers. I did not want to be labelled as a 'sappy' writer, especially when faced with works addressing serious world issues; heartbreak felt irrelevant. However, writing about this exact fear helped eradicate it completely. It was my turn to join a line of poets occupied with matters of the heart and offer my perspective. What an honour.

Studying Flaubert's *Madame Bovary* at university familiarised me with 'le mot juste': the right word. I might change one word in a poem months after writing it, obsessed with achieving my understanding of the perfect portrayal of a subject. It may change again once circumstances in my life shift, exposing me to more experience and understanding, thus disqualifying my previous choice of noun, adjective or verb as the 'right one'. It was a challenge leaving this behind, accepting that my poetry is a snapshot of time, and not a constant promise of understanding as I grow and change. Perhaps poems which no longer resonate with me will mean something to other readers.

'Wonky Fingers': I do actually have fingers that bend the wrong way and it is those fingers that scribbled every poem in this book. The experience of frantically blurting inky ideas onto a page is unmatched. Excitedly mind-mapping, crossing things out and seeing how words feel to write, say and touch. I am delighted that something beautiful has sprung from an amalgamation of bones at the end of my arm. Ultimately, I hope my poems can be annotated, analysed and broken down into so many pieces that when rebuilt, they mean something completely different. It is my intention that my words are reborn, relearnt and live a hundred different lives.

Raiding The Honey Pot

1

Sweetness begins like the drizzling of a
raincloud
Sporadically spitting in tasteful bursts
Like ink blotches on wet parchment
Sugar waltzes with taste buds and
Bides its time before bursting the dam
And flooding the mouth with ambrosia

Pray the bees do not mind.

The Colour of Passion

Red, a child would say, surpassing the interest of
Scarlet and crimson. Burgundy or blood.
An ancient would declare the colour of passion is but the
Creamy contours of the sands of passing and the desert of time.
A mother would croon the hue of passion is the saxe field her children adore:
The speckled cobalt of the night
Buried, Patroclus caresses a figment of passion - the
Sandy soles of Achilles heels

So you ask me… is passion not but love?
Aye, but passion is greedy.
Demands the force of seven suns, a googolplex of galaxies and
Heart, strong as a Roman league
So you ask me… is passion not but strength?
Nay, passion is a poison, a pestilence, the seduction of a spider's web
An ancient chides you, Shakespeare warned you
For "I am not what I am."

Gold. Burning, churning. The glint of hatred, the
abuse of the sun and the colour of Circe's magic
Blue. Or rather a kaleidoscope shattered with
shards of lazuli and fire.
Fire! Is there no paint to create the scalding,
sizzling, carnivorous heat?
Though I was speaking of ice

So you ask me… is passion not but pain?
So I answer, my child, my love, my friend, my
student
My passion is petrichor
The musky browns of romance, coffee and sand
after rain
The beige of parchment and images of my ink

At the end of the road
We greet the obsidian abyss
And so comes my time to ask too
My child, my love, my friend, my student,
Is passion not but the colour of you?

A Trio of Haikus

4

Drooping Lilies
Count ninety-nine doors,
Each with a Hera petal
Shredded on the floor

Amazing Grace
How sweet the sound is
Of discordant song - fearful
Of disgracing God

Losing Sunlight
When looking at stars,
Bright and shining horizons
Burn as fast as hope

Earthling

5

Rancid odours rake over me. Damp wood
becomes damper yet,
Mould takes stake, spreading like frost over a
still lake.
Mother mixes the earthy dough, churning deeper
and
Deeper.
An oven-warmed tray lies there for me,
Delivering back to the womb of the world.

Rain in The Gallery

The tranquility of the museum satiates the girl in
front of the painting
A marble colosseum colliding with the auburn
calamity of deft brush strokes
Queries of loss and heat rather than a certitude
of massacre and flame.
Does the sun rise on The Slave Ship?
Blurring contours of piano keys follow the girl
through the gallery. Clair de Lune:
Clarity's antonym in a whorl of pedalling and
parallel figures. The drum of fingers on keys like
an
Impression of ballerina feet on wooden floors,
laden with legacies of dancers. Composed in
elegance and grace.
The girl in the gallery turns her head. To the
pitter-patter of rain outside the window, and the
obscurity granted to the wide outside.

The art gallery, for all its phenomena, does not
compare to the unified surrendering of our
digitised lenses.
An entire ecosystem habitually blurred by the
machine imitation of the perfected human eye.

And yet the rain blurs the camera and it must
fall.
The girl dons a raincoat. The girl in the raincoat
relishes in the magnetism of rain.
A human proclivity to smell the damp dust in the
air and feel-

The girl in the raincoat feels more than the pull
of vapour from clouds.
A pull of tears from glands, and cosmetics from
pores. A pull of kohl from weighted lashes. The
pull of gravity, streaking black down the girl's
face. Art.
Emotions impalpable, as raindrops merge so
thoroughly with tears that even the girl in the
raincoat cannot
Distinguish empyrean anguish from an ache so
pure and heartfelt and human.
Or is it joy? The impressionists can debate.

With military precision, the 'rise of the
umbrellas' is upon us. Laughable
Attempts to disregard the exigency of weather.
As if the persistent percussion wouldn't remain
on the canopy.
As if it wouldn't streak the raincoats and soles of
its victims, of its victors.

The girl with the umbrella accommodates these
offerings within her abode, a dragon-hoard of
whispered rhymes about water from the sky
Does she know the prescription for tribulation?
A hot chocolate, a seat at a window and a deluge
to tend all plagues.

The girl at the window is not truly there.
Positioned as an impression of presence, she
becomes the voyeur of The Shipwreck In The
Desert: a scene so dry and melancholy.
If only the bedouin could see the sky grey and
clouds morph, pregnant with hope.
Rain, in the heat of the desert: a blessed notice to
prostrate and cry 'الحمد الله'
All praise be to God. For mercy, for rain so
simple and surplus.
The girl in the desert returns to the sanctity of
the dripping present.

For some, rain is the grim reaper chaperoning
the advancing monsoon.
For every girl in the gallery, in the rain, at the
window, there must be a boy in the debris, with
a fever, in the hearse.
The shimmering seeds that cascade know no
virtue or mercy, burdened with no moral duty.
They become us. Through all our devastation
and fairness, sculpting the human condition.

Birthed, just like the girl in the rain, as part of a
sentient continuum.

The heavens have opened, say the great writers,
and with it - everything

P.S. - don't forget the puddles!
Sincerely, the girl in the wellies, living in silver
linings

A Sister's Lament

Brother of mine, become the eternal muse
Of a blue mourning tune
Give me a full bouquet to set down and plant
At the cross beneath which you humbly lay
Answer to my conflict with the tragic
Injustice of circumstance
It doesn't get easier.

Widowed Roses

Aphrodisiac is much too lovely
A word to meddle in sex and rock n' roll.
Its eloping consonants conjure
Chronicles of lovers and the soul.

Whispered comforts seek the melodrama
Of two wilting roses on the edge
Of the world without a breeze to pollinate
The blossoming Petrarchan hedge.
It is birthed of literature suckled on
Bleeding hearts and crumbling headstones.
So grieve, dearest widows and widowers;
Find peace in the arms of poetry.
Lie still in the wake of Shakespeare's
apothecary:
A toast to Aphrodite, and "thus with a kiss I die"

No Sweeter Canvas Than I

12

Pastel purples and affectionate browns pepper
my collarbone
They lace up my neck and nape in an ardent
arrangement
It is artful.
At the valley of my breasts, initials stain my skin
At the curve of my thighs, crescent moons are
imprinted into the fabric of my frame
Bathed in your pigments, I most contently
become your canvas

Bear Witness To Human Connection

Do you ever think about the opinions of dust
motes hanging heavy in the air?
Whether they whisper to one another about the
taste of our skin or the damp veil of our sweat
Perhaps we divulge the same particles when
breathing the stale air of the abandoned church.
Perhaps the dust motes scribe the same secret
prayer.
Am I giving you my breath? And in doing so, do
you become my lung? Become one?
But we do indeed become one when the sun sets
and the silent dust motes settle to witness human
connection.
How long have they been here? Are they
immortal, like tragedy, or do they live and
breathe, and relive and flee, like caterpillars
turning into butterflies?
Where has my mind gone - running with the
possibilities of dust motes? How shameful in the
face of human connection.
One last question then: Were they there in the
beginning, singing with the angels?
Celestial conduits of human sanctity

The Formalities of Leaving

Shut the door on your way out,
My love. I do not want chilling gusts of your
Next conquests. It will darken my craft and
crafting.
It will erase the neons and pastels that make up
My poetry and I.
How I miss the artwork you left on my skin,
My dearest. It is so pale now. It is so bland.

How to press flowers (for poets) in less than eight steps

1. Acquire a flower - most preferably one with sentimental value, otherwise why are you even bothering. You need emotion to motivate writing.

2. Spread out each petal so that it lays flat on the tissue paper. Make sure the stem is gone because why on earth would you press a stem. Unless you are composing an Ode to Thorns, paired with the poetic balance of beauty and pain. Be still my heart.

3. Cover both sides of the flower with the tissue paper in order to soak up the fluid. Whilst doing so, formulate a simile about the tissue soaking up the lifeblood of the flower like the pillow soaks up your tears every night. Find other love-sick examples on the world-wide-web.

4. Place the flower in a tight vice, or for regular people, under a stack of heavy books. The flower will bleed into their pages like its sentiment into my memory. Make up your own sappy lines.

5. Leave it untouched for (a very long) two weeks in order for it to dry out. Contemplate the ins and outs of floral imagery, fricative lexical patterns and tripartite lists during this time.

6. Be very delicate when uncovering it and laying it out, for it may disintegrate. Place a pin in the middle of the flower to secure all the petals. No deserters. This is a good time to mention the fragility of dead things.

7. Frame it. Hide it. Burn it. I don't care as long as you promise to write about pressing matters, pressing flowers.

Say A Little Prayer For You

May God preserve the render of you in my
memory,
for I have crafted and perfected not only your
image,
but the very essence of your character.
Meticulous in my work, recalling even the echo
And cadence of forgotten laughter.

The good in you, though lost, lives on here.

Puddles and Petrichor

The surface runs away from me
And suddenly, the unfinished letters,
Unwashed plates and unswept floors
Are of the utmost importance.
I will never get to smell sand after rain;
Virgin parchments I will never touch
Make the trial of breaching the water's tension
Tantalising. Possible. Right there.

But there is no breeze here;
No yellow, red or suffocating green.
The scene is blue, and the silver is weaning.
The bubbles are smaller now - like pebbles in a
canyon,
Like breath on a glass, I fade now
Into the deep…

disclaimer: sad girl poet

Forgive me for the aesthetic, all lowercase title
I'm scared that I will fall into the stereotypical
role of the sad girl poet
With all this teenage angst and heartbreak ebbed
into formulaic rhyme

How do my eulogies for love compare to the
demand for groundbreaking stanzas?
Adventure in verse into the deserts of political
discontent,
Campaigners for the persecution of mother
nature or
Iambic commentaries on the epic faults of
consumerism and materialism and imperialism
and capitalism and communism
And I am running out of breath.
Forgive me for fulfilling empty pages with sad
girl poetry

Bring on the electric guitar and the pop rock
lyrics about how Lothario has ruined me
I look up from the pen
It has started to form an ink blot on the page as I
contemplate my descent into a career as the sad
girl poet

I am not a refugee, nor a charitable volunteer.
I am not a victim of war, or a sufferer of disease.
I am not a mother and cannot tell you of the
gravitational shift a child conjures.
I birth only poetry.
With an air of melodrama I profess that
The sole beauty of my agony resides in rhyme,
Whilst lyrical respites for my inarticulate
turbulence mellow the surmounting pressure of
loving.

Is this where I find my purpose? My 'poetic
voice' - preached by editors and publishers alike.
An incalculable hypothesis of whether the public
will care about the beauty I find in
Bees and honey
Or the tiny bubbles you see when exhaling
underwater.
Will they appreciate my translation of a thesis
literature has already drowned in?

I will be the sad girl poet, who relishes in the
space between words and the
Longing in weighted pauses.
I will be another in a long line of writers who
just has to redefine heartbreak.
At the very least, my sad girl poetry is honest,
all-mine and undeniably in love.

Loving Intangibly

I thought there was no more romantic a phrase
than:
I love you more than anything
Until you responded
I love you more than everything
And took my breath away - my very
understanding of
Language and lexical expectation decimated.

Was it that I loved you in potential?
And so, if you reciprocated in the here and now,
Making our culmination so very tangible…
Why is it that I am still loving hypothetically?

I told Shelley about my lover

I met a traveller from an antique land
Weighted with whispers of the fractured
Ozymandius.
And when asked of my tale,
I replied:
"It was the kind of love where we danced in
empty parks,
Under moonlight and to the euphonious beats of
our hearts."
Far greater an adventure than a pilgrimage to the
King of Kings

Refuge

23

Dust rains and the teardrops stain
The birdsong dies
In another world, wine spills and
Telephone bills litter the bedroom floor

It goes on, all while infants scream
Dust settles on fields of court
Crows cry upon the stones
Blanketing mothers and daughters
Enveloping fathers and sons

Victorian Time of Year

How many times has the tale of autumn
been tongued by story-tellers far and wide.
The son of the Sun in the leaves in the morning
Mourning the sleek, crisp greens of June and
fruits of May
Leaves into paper, stained with ink, smothered in
meaning.
Every other author setting the scene in
September, October, November
Every other teacher preaching the meaning of
autumn: decay
Death of the leaves in the trees, with wrinkles
and crinkles.
"Heave!" Say the ants on the forest floors,
preparing the fort for winter.

In Love With The Inanimate

It is easier to be in love with hatred, than
negligence

I am in love with my piano, my bookshelf and
inky blotches I leave behind when scribbling

I am in love with chocolate melting on my
tongue and the way raspberry ice cream leaves
residue on my lips

So that you may taste it when you kiss me

Are you in love with the way I taste without
raspberry? Salty, sweet, saccharine.

Sweat for passion, tears for longing and blood
for when my lips need reddening but raspberry
ice cream isn't available

I am in love with the grass on which you took
me; the dirt that branded my fingernails

I am in love with the sound of my poetry on
your lips. I am no longer my own

List of Things That Matter:

1. Lemon and Mint
2. Old Bookshops
3. My toaster that always burns my toast
4. The deleted stanza from 'Rain in The Gallery'
5. My hatred for referencing
6. The beginning of Arabic fairytales
كان يا مكان في قديم الزمان
Once upon a time, in a land far away
7. The phrases "coveted moonlight" and
"sustained eccentricity"
8. A sweet cup of tea
9. People who manage to sleep in airports in
incomprehensible positions
10. The rebirth and relearning of poetry

Note To You: Messy and Unfinished

Dear Reader (singular),

Slanted, vivacious, honest. I have written you
many a letter, and yet how ironic it is that the
last I write to you is
Rigid, impartial, censored in a book of poetry.
The spaces between words, the things I haven't
said inhale us and exhale you.
I am left trapped inside the husk, spectator to the
gangrene of my will. It reminds me of how you
made me watch you. On her.
Manuscript: a hull of a story - rendered chapters
neighbouring the volumes on my bookshelf.
Never fear dying, for my writing does not decay.
Uncanny in the rocking chair, my vow of
independence shamed by the second cup of tea
that must go cold. Oh - promises - how
Admirably noble - so hearty underneath lovers'
bodies - breathed into the atmosphere and
diffused with expectation, left to exist as a
whisper unweighted by rain.
Exemplar constitutions of how much one could
love, or could dedicate, or could fight to stay.

It is with hope, sparser than found in promises,
that you will read this and understand.
"Darling" - a word like a lover dipping her in an
old dance, then tactfully sweeping her up - as if
ever letting her fall was an option.
Where was my darling when I plummeted and
was not silent?
Naïve was I to think you adored my cries.
May I wish you well? I don't. May you struggle
through many Januarys.
Perhaps I am rambling now. Wonky fingers do
make effective proclamations, though cryptic.
I grew them back from bone and dust myself,
like puzzle pieces rearranged to make a picture
that will no longer weep.

Ever-loving,
Sarah

ACKNOWLEDGEMENT

I want to express my deep appreciation to my mother, who never doubted me, who was patient when I was frustrated and eager when I was idle. I love you. To my father, who was the first to hear my new poetry and who loves me beyond the English and Arabic languages.

Thank you dearly, Emma-Jane Weighell, who told me in so many words that it is always better to be kind and hurt, than cruel and untroubled.

Thank you to Emile Moriette-Sala, for your exquisite book cover. It is a privilege to have your artwork be part of my poetry.

This book could not have been written without the unwavering confidence of my best friends, Amani Rafiq and Molly-Jane Bradley, who looked after my heart for months. And most notably, thank you to Shania Mehta, who sat next to me in Psychology everyday of the week, watched me write, asked me about my progress, condemned those who inspired my writing, and still insists on a signed copy.

This collection would not exist if I was left to my own devices, but I do want to thank younger-Sarah. She sat down with conviction on the 31st of January 2023 and promised to write, whether that be for spite, love or healing. I am proud of you.